MONEY AND BANKS

by Donald R. German

illustrated by Tomás Gonzales

DANDELION BOOKS
Published by Dandelion Press, Inc.

MONEY

Before there was such a thing as money, people traded for things they needed. This is called the *barter system*, and it doesn't work very well. A farmer, for example, might trade a chicken for a pair of shoes. But what if the shoemaker didn't like chicken? And how could he give change in shoes?

To make the transfer of goods and services easy, people need a *medium of exchange*. A medium of exchange is something of agreed value that can be used to pay for things. Salt was an early medium of exchange because it was very valuable in ancient days. Our modern word *salary* comes from the Latin word *salarium*, which means salt money. When an item such as salt is used as a medium of exchange, it is called *commodity money*, because the item, or commodity, can be exchanged for other things and can also be used itself. There are many interesting examples of commodity money. At one time, the Eskimos used fishhooks as a medium of exchange. In colonial Virginia, tobacco was used. In early New England, nails and bushels

of corn were used as money. And in ancient China, small knives were used. This eventually led to the curious custom of making Chinese coins with strange little tails to represent what had once been knife blades.

Commodity money didn't work very well either, however, for two reasons. First of all, things may lose their value as times change. If nails are the medium of exchange, for example, when people don't need any new buildings they won't value nails as much as before, so nails won't work as money. Second, it is hard to place a set value on certain items. If cows are used as a medium of exchange, obviously a healthy, strong cow is worth a lot more than a little, scrawny one. But how much more?

Representative money, therefore, was the next step in making a more useful medium of exchange. If everyone agreed that a certain representative item had a given value, then it could be exchanged for goods or services as needed even though it had no other use. The most spectacular type of representative money was used many years ago on the island of Yap. Giant doughnut-shaped flat stones that often weighed many tons were the medium of exchange. Some

American Indians used *wampumpeag*, which were cylindrical beads made from shells that had been polished, pierced, and strung. Black or dark purple beads were especially valued. But there were problems here, too. Among the Indians who used wampum, everyone wanted the pretty strung shells even though they had no real value. A clever workman could make a lot of wampum and get rich even though he did not make anything that was actually useful to his tribe.

Ideally, money should have certain characteristics. It should be made in specified quantities by an authorized government. It should last a long time. It should all be of a standard kind. It should be of a set value. It should be easy to carry. And it should be capable of being divided so that change can easily be made.

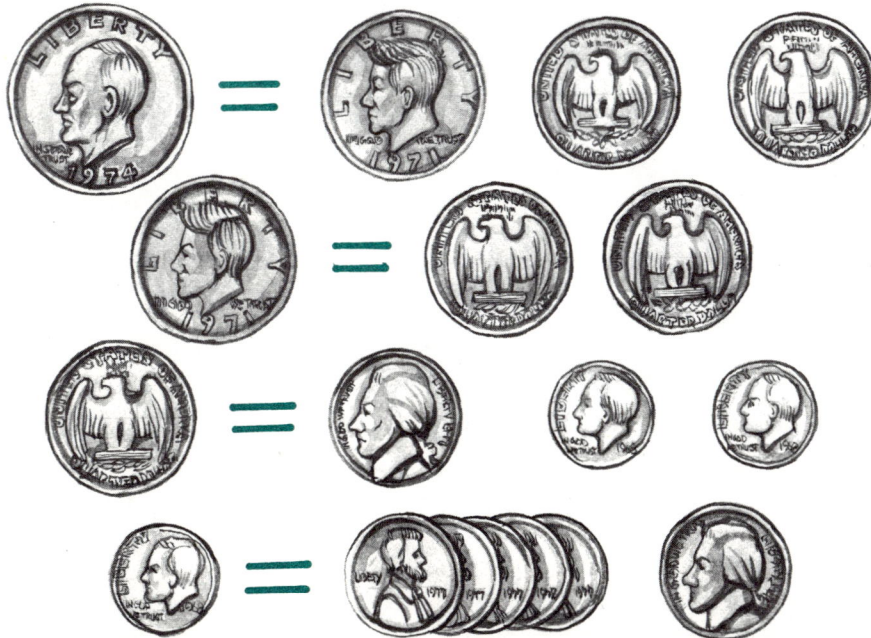

Money as we know it today started almost 3,000 years ago in Lydia, an ancient country in Asia Minor that is now a part of Turkey. The Lydians made the first coins.

A coin is a piece of metal stamped with the authority of the government as a guarantee of its value. A great idea! With coins, the farmer could sell his eggs and chickens to everyone in town, and they could pay him with a standard medium of exchange. In turn, he could buy shoes or pants or whatever he needed. And the shoemaker who didn't like chicken could take the farmer's coins and buy himself whatever he wished.

But even coins had disadvantages. For one thing, they can get pretty heavy to lug around when you have a considerable sum. The answer to this problem came in 1640 when King Charles I of England went broke!

Until that time, London merchants put their gold coins in the famous Tower of London for safekeeping. But, when the king ran out of money and no one would lend him any, he seized the Tower and took the gold. Naturally, the merchants were very upset. So they offered to lend King Charles £40,000 if he would give back their gold.

When they got it back, they gave it for safekeeping to goldsmiths, men who made jewelry and other objects out of gold and who had sturdy vaults in which to protect the precious metal. The goldsmiths gave the merchants receipts for the money they held. And pretty soon the merchants found it easier to simply spend the receipts than to go to the goldsmith, take out the gold, and give it to another merchant who would only take it back to the goldsmith anyway. Thus *currency*, or paper money, came into being.

The money in our country was once made of gold and silver. Then, for large amounts, the government issued "gold certificates" and "silver certificates" which could be taken to a bank and redeemed for real gold and silver. However, because these metals are scarce, there simply isn't a large enough supply to redeem all our money, so most modern currency consists of Federal Reserve Notes which are issued by government authorization and backed by the vast assets of the Federal Reserve Banks. And our coins, issued by the United States Mint, are metal "sandwiches" of copper between two slices of nickel alloy.

A lot of American history is portrayed on our coins and bills. George Washington, our first president, is on both the quarter and the $1 bill. And Abraham Lincoln, sixteenth president of the United States, who led the country through the Civil War, is on both the penny and the $5 bill. Other presidents whose portraits are on our money are Thomas Jefferson, who appears on the nickel and the $2 bill; Franklin D. Roosevelt on the dime; John F. Kennedy on the half

dollar; Dwight D. Eisenhower on the $1 coin; Andrew Jackson on the $20 bill; and Ulysses S. Grant on the $50 bill. Only two persons who were not presidents are pictured: Alexander Hamilton, first secretary of the Treasury, who is on the $10 bill, and Benjamin Franklin, the most famous diplomat during the American Revolution, who is on the $100 bill. Soon a new coin will be minted—a smaller $1 coin.

Historical figures were not used on all of our money, however. During the Civil War when metal was scarce, the U.S. Treasury issued 500,000 five-cent notes. The picture on these notes was that of a man named Spencer M. Clark. Everyone was mystified. Who was Mr. Clark? Certainly not a past president. And not a famous hero or statesman. It was discovered that he was the chief clerk of the National Currency Division of the Treasury. And he had put his own portrait on the notes. Congress was furious! Ever since then it has been the law that, in order to be pictured on U.S. currency, a person must be famous—and dead!

FIR8T NATIONAL
BANK & TRUST

January 4, 19 79

CHECK
NUMBER
5

PAY TO THE
ORDER OF *The Book shop* $ *10.00*

AMOUNT *Ten dollars and zero hundredths*

John Doe

Actually, most of the "money" we spend isn't really money at all. At least, not in the sense of bills or coins. Our government simply couldn't print enough bills to take care of our needs if everything were paid for in cash. So people literally make their own money by writing checks. The person who writes the check has a deduction made from his bank account, and the person who receives the check has his account increased; no actual currency changes hands.

Credit cards have been called "plastic money," and the name is a good one. With the aid of computers, charges against a person's credit are accumulated and then paid, usually by check, when he or she receives a monthly bill. What a long way we've come since the shoemaker had to eat chicken if he wanted to sell shoes!

BANKS

Banks specialize in handling money. They are equipped with vaults that are safe from fire, thieves, and even plain carelessness. And they make life easier for people by simplifying the handling of their financial affairs.

Like money, banks have their roots well back in history. In ancient Egypt, which had a highly developed civilization, there was no such thing as money. Yet a kind of banking based on an elaborate barter system existed there about 1,000 years before the first coins were made in nearby Lydia.

About 4,000 years ago, the first known financial institutions to resemble modern banks began in Babylon and were run by the priests in the religious temples. And the first real bank also started in Babylon about 2,500 years ago. Called the Igibi, it made loans on objects that were held as security, took money on deposit and paid interest on it, and even made loans on crops that were yet to be raised.

As people used money more and more, the need for banks and bank services spread. Our word "bank" comes from the Italian word *banca*, which referred to the bench on which medieval moneychangers stacked their coins. But a modern bank doesn't look much like a moneychanger's bench. The building may be big and imposing, or it may, at least from the outside, look something like a store in a shopping center. Whatever its appearance, when you go into a bank you will notice that the people who work there are arranged so that they can easily help you.

The most noticeable people who work in a bank are the *tellers*. The name "teller" comes from a Dutch word, *tellen*, which means "to count." And that is what tellers do. They take in the money people deposit, pay out the money people withdraw, cash checks, and do almost all of the actual money-counting operations in a bank. Being a teller is a responsible job that requires accuracy and personal honesty. Just forty years ago, most bank tellers were men. But today, over eighty percent of the tellers in our country are women.

Another person you'll notice in many banks is sitting behind a desk near the door where it is easy for people coming into the bank for the first time to get help. This person is called a new-account clerk, or a service representative, or something similar. He or she opens new accounts and explains the bank's services.

Farther back in the office, where it is usually more private, you'll see one or more people sitting at desks. They are called loan officers and they lend money to people who need it for all sorts of reasons.

Banks need officers who are allowed to sign legal papers on behalf of the bank. And because banks have so many documents to handle, they have more officers than some other businesses. People most often deal with the branch or office manager.

And, finally, behind the scenes, many other bank workers keep records, run giant computers, send checks to other banks, and study ways in which the bank can help people in the community.

It is important to remember that all of that money you see in a bank and the millions of dollars the bank advertises it has as assets don't belong to the bank. The dollars belong to its depositors—people just like you. The bank keeps those dollars safe for its depositors and, at the same time, pools the money to lend to people and businesses in the community. These people and businesses pay the bank *interest* for the use of the money. In turn, this interest is used to pay *savings interest* to the bank's depositors; it is also used for the salaries of the people who work for the bank, and for the expenses of running the buildings and equipment.

WHAT A BANK CAN DO FOR YOU

Savings accounts are among the oldest of banking services. Here's how they work. You open a savings account by signing a *signature card* and making a deposit of money at your bank. The bank then gives you a small *passbook* that shows the account is open in your

name and the amount of money you have on deposit. Every time you make another deposit, the teller takes the passbook and, on a special machine, adds in the new amount so that the balance in the account is always accurate. Also, whenever you wish, you may make a withdrawal—that is, take money out of the account, right up to the amount of the balance; that is shown in your passbook, too.

DEPOSITOR'S NAME ON PAGE ONE

	DATE	WITHDRAWAL	DEPOSIT	INTEREST	BALANCE
1	5 Jan.		100.00		100.00
2	31 Dec.			5.00	105.00
3					
4					

Frequently, the teller takes the passbook and adds on an extra sum of money. This is called *savings interest*, and it is money the bank pays you in return for using your money. In a typical savings account, a bank pays you about $5 every year for every $100 you have on deposit.

Checking accounts started in somewhat the same way that paper money did. Hundreds of years ago, merchants discovered that they could pay for things without risk of being robbed or losing their money if they just wrote other merchants a note to take to the goldsmith who kept their money in his vaults. That's all a check is — a note telling the bank to pay some of the money you have on deposit to the person you wish paid.

```
┌─────────────────────────────────────────────┐
│  BANK'S                                       │
│   NAME              DATE  Jan 4, 19 79        │
│                                               │
│  PAY TO  The Bookshop            $ 10.00      │
│                                               │
│  AMOUNT  ten dollars and zero hundreths       │
│                                               │
│           SIGNATURE  John Fox                 │
│                                               │
└─────────────────────────────────────────────┘
```

All that is required when a person writes a check is that he actually have money in the bank and that he follow a basic legal form. This includes a date, the amount of money, a bank at which the check can be paid, the name of the person to whom the money should be given, and the signature of the person writing the check on his or her account.

Most checks are printed on paper following strict legal forms, complete with special numbers in magnetic ink that activate the bank's computer. But banks can accept other objects as checks if all of the information required is written on them. As a joke, checks have been written on some strange objects. Angry citizens, for example, have written checks for tax payments on shirts with a note saying, "You're taking the shirt off of my back!" Checks have even been written on clamshells, and, on a popular TV show, a check made out to a charity was written on the bare back of a pretty model in a bathing suit! Although they were strange, these checks were perfectly good.

Everyone can open a savings account, but only adults can have checking accounts because of the legal requirements. Opening a checking account, however, is pretty much like opening a savings account. The customer signs a signature card, makes a deposit, and receives a supply of checks along with a little booklet, called a *check register*, in which he or she can keep an accurate record of the account by adding in all of the deposits and subtracting all of the checks

CHECK NO.	DATE	CHECKS ISSUED TO OR DESCRIPTION OF DEPOSIT	(−) AMOUNT OF CHECK	(+) AMOUNT OF DEPOSIT	BALANCE
					100 00
	1/3	Deposit (cash)		50 00	+ 50 00
					150 00
5	1/4	The Bookshop	10 00		− 10 00
					140 00

written. Some people keep their personal records on check *stubs*, small pieces of paper that remain in the checkbook after the checks have been torn out. Every month, the bank sends the customer a *statement*, which is a copy of the records for that account kept by the bank's computer or bookkeeping machine. By comparing the statement with the check register, the customer can be sure just how much money is in the account and see if he or she, or the bank, has made any errors.

Banks use the money their customers deposit to make *loans*. The most important loan most people make is a *mortgage* loan to buy a house. Houses cost a great deal of money, and not many people can just go and buy one. A mortgage loan lets a family own and live in a house while they pay back the money they borrowed to buy it.

Another popular loan is an *automobile* loan. Although they cost less than houses, cars cost a lot of money, so an auto loan allows a person to own and enjoy a car while paying for it out of his or her regular earnings.

People borrow for all sorts of reasons. Some are happy reasons, such as to take a trip to an exciting foreign country or to buy a new boat. Some are sad reasons, such as to pay medical bills or even funeral expenses. Banks lend people money for any worthwhile purpose—but only if they can repay the money. After all, it belongs to the bank's depositors, and the bank is watching out for them. So to borrow money, a person needs a steady source of income, usually a good job. And he or she needs to have a record of having paid bills on time. For a very large loan, the person may also need *collateral*, which is simply an item of value that can be sold for money to repay the loan if something should go wrong. In a mortgage loan, the collateral is the house itself; but for some loans, stocks or bonds may be pledged as collateral.

Banks make loans to *businesses* as well as to individuals. Stores borrow money to buy extra merchandise at certain times of the year when they do more business, such as at Christmas and back-to-school time. Factories borrow to buy huge pieces of machinery, and can use the money the machinery helps them earn in order to pay back the loan. In fact, businesses borrow to buy everything from airplanes to zinc! Some business loans are so large that a single bank can't risk that much money to one borrower, so several banks will each lend a portion of the money. Business loans help factories to make the goods we all need and help stores to stock them. And then individual loans, including credit cards, help people to buy those goods.

Another service that banks offer is providing safe deposit boxes. Like savings accounts, safe deposit service is very ancient, dating back thousands of years. For a very small sum of money, usually just a few dollars a year, a bank will rent a customer a private little vault inside the bank's big burglarproof, fireproof, lossproof vault. No one, not even a bank officer, is allowed to open a safe deposit box except the customer who rents it. Safe deposit boxes are the ideal place to keep all of the important papers a family eventually collects, such as marriage and birth certificates, wills, deeds to the house, and legal papers.

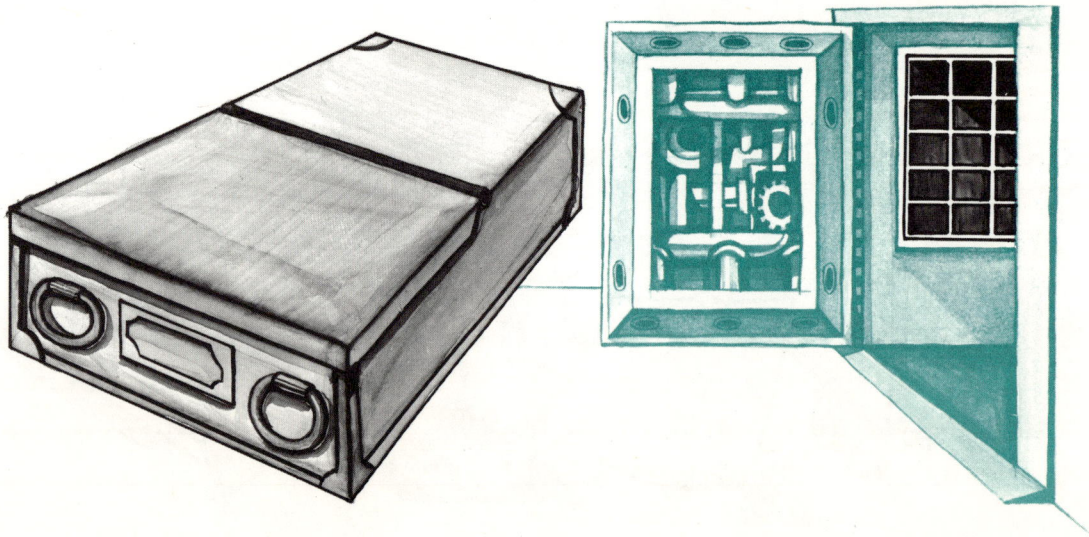

Money and banks are pretty important to all of us and to our communities. The next time you spend a quarter, stop and think. The money you give the storekeeper helps to pay for the item you bought. And a small amount, his profit, helps to pay the store rent, the electric bill, the phone bill, and even goes to buy the food the storekeeper's family eats. The money you spend helps make jobs in your community. And when all of the people in your community buy from each other, it helps everyone to prosper.

But don't think that you should spend *all* your money in order to help your community. Saving in a bank will help, too. Your dollars will help you by earning interest, and they will also be put to work right in your hometown.

Next time you take a long walk through your neighborhood, look around . . . . Perhaps the dollars you and your friends saved, or the money your parents and their friends have in the bank, went to help that new storekeeper start a business. In turn, the money he or she earns will create jobs in your community, and the business will pay taxes to help pay for your school, and for fire and police protection for everyone.

And when you see an older friend drive a new car, realize that it

was probably made possible by a loan from the bank where money from many, many depositors was pooled together so that loans could be made to people who needed them.

Take a look around your own house, too. Chances are it was paid for with a mortgage loan made to your parents if they own it, or to your landlord if your family pays rent.

Banks pool money for the common good—and with safety. In addition to a strong vault and careful lending policies, bank deposits are insured by agencies of the government so that your dollars are really safe.

It's pretty impressive, isn't it? Especially considering that it all started with shoemakers who didn't like chicken!

A GUIDE TO THE COVER

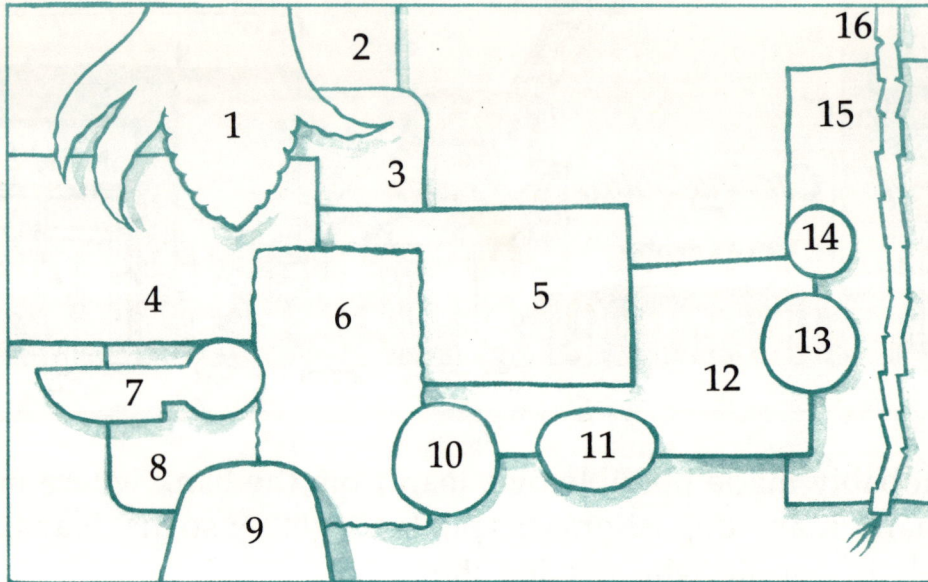

1. Corn
2. Mortgage agreement
3. Savings account passbook
4. Spencer M. Clark note
5. Personal check
6. American colonial currency
7. Chinese knife money
8. Credit card
9. Babylonian receipt written on clay
10. Early U.S. gold coin
11. Early Lydian coin
12. Modern U.S. dollar bill
13. Roman copper coin
14. Modern Canadian cent
15. Goldsmith's receipt
16. Wampumpeag